Convoy

CAROLINE DAVIES

INDEPENDENT INNOVATIVE INTERNATIONAL

Published by Cinnamon Press
Meirion House,
Glan yr afon,
Tanygrisiau,
Blaenau Ffestiniog,
Gwynedd,
LL41 3SU
www.cinnamonpress.com

ISBN: 978-1-907090-85-1

British Library Cataloguing in Publication Data. A CIP record for this book can be obtained from the British Library.

Designed and typeset in Palatino by Cinnamon Press
Cover from original artwork - photograph by Sergeant Bill Lazell, Copyright © Paul Lazell
Cover design by Jan Fortune

Printed in Poland

Cinnamon Press is represented in the UK by Inpress Ltd www.inpressbooks.co.uk and in Wales by the Welsh Books Council www.cllc.org.uk

Acknowledgments

This book would not have been written were it not for my grandfather, Jim Honeybill and all the men who served on the merchant ships supplying Malta during the war. It is also written for my mother, who awakened my interest in poems and stories when I was a child and who told me a little about what it was like growing up during the war.

I would like to thank Jan Fortune who believed in the book from its early stages and a special thank you to Vanessa Gebbie who has been a staunch source of support all the way through.

I thank Paul Lazell who provided the photograph for the cover and also allowed me to read his diary of his father Sergeant Bill Lazell who was stationed on Malta with the Royal Artillery. Many thanks go to Tom Neil for his book *Onward to Malta* and for kindly saying he didn't mind me turning some of his experiences into poems. Pete Marshall not only provided a retreat at Tyn-y-Coed for the times when I needed to get on with the writing but also introduced me to his father John who was with the Blue Funnel line and sailed with the Ajax after the war. John gave me insights into life at sea and was meticulous in commenting on the maritime aspects of the poems. Any mistakes, which remain, are due entirely to my misunderstandings.

I am grateful to Katy Evans-Bush, who saw the book through the final stages.

A number of books were my constant companions during the writing of this collection including Richard Woodman's *Malta Convoys*, Tom Neil's *Onward to Malta*, Ian Cameron's

Red Duster, White Ensign, Roger Hill's *Destroyer Captain,* Max Arthur's *Lost Voices of the Royal Navy,* James Holland's *Fortress Malta,* Captain S W Roskill's *A Merchant Fleet at War 1939:1945,* Peter C Smith's *Pedestal The Convoy that saved Malta,* Laddie Lucas' *Malta: The Thorn in Rommel's side,* Geoffrey Wellum's *First Light,* Patrick Gibb's *Torpedo Leader on Malta,* Lord James Douglas Hamilton's *The Air Battle for Malta,* Peter Shankland and Anthony Hunter's *Malta Convoy,* Tim Johnston's *Tattered Battlements,* William J Lewis' *Under the red duster: the Merchant Navy in World War II,* Michael Pearson's *The Ohio and Malta* and Woody Woodhall's *Soldier, Sailor and Airman too.*

Thank you to my local writers group for the discussions about poems and other literary matters, Judi Moore, Guy Russell, Ruth Downie, Jan Lowell, Kathy Barbour, Chris Allen, Carol Barac and Neil Beardmore. Thanks also to Josh Lanyon who provided encouragement at the eleventh hour.

Finally and most importantly my love and gratitude to Seán, and my sons Luke and Ciarán who have tolerated my preoccupations with merchant ships and Malta with good grace.

Contents

List of Ships

Aagtekirk: Dutch freighter
MV Ajax: Blue Funnel Line
       Captain John R Scott, Jim Honeybill, Lt P Aylwin
SS Almeria Lykes: Lykes Steamship Co
Ancient: A tug
HMS Arethusa: A Cruiser
HMS Argus: An Aircraft carrier
HMS Ark Royal: An Aircraft carrier
SS Avila Star: Blue Star Line
Bhutan: Hain Steamship Co Ltd
HMS Bramham: A Destroyer
       Lt Edward 'Eddie' F Baines
MV Brisbane Star: Blue Star line
       Captain Fred N Riley
HMS Cairo: A cruiser
HMS Charybis:A cruiser
SS City of Calcutta: Ellerman lines
SS City of Pretoria: Ellerman lines
SS Clan Ferguson: Clan Line
HMS Cossack: A destroyer
MV Deucalion: Blue Funnel line
       Captain Ramsey Brown, Carpenter Norman W Owen
M V Dorset: Federal Steam Navigation Company
       Captain J C Tuckett, Apprentice Desmond Dickens
SS Durham: Federal Steam Navigation Co
HMS Eagle: An Aircraft carrier

       Henry Rathbone, Visual Signals Rating

HMS Edinburgh: A Cruiser
MV Empire Hope: Shaw, Savill and Albion Co
       Jim Perry
HMS Furious: An Aircraft carrier
MV Glenorchy: Blue Funnel Line
       Captain G Leslie, 2nd mate BH Skilling,
       3rd mate R M Simon.
HMS Indomitable: An Aircraft carrier
       Captain Thomas Troubridge
HNLMS Jacob Van Heemskerck: Royal Netherlands Navy cruiser
HMS Jaunty: A Tug
HMS Ledbury: A Destroyer
       Lt Commander Roger Hill
Leinster: An Irish sea ferry also used as a troopship

HMS Manchester: A Cruiser
M V Melbourne Star: Blue Star Line
        Captain David R MacFarlane
HMS Nelson: A Battleship
        Flagship of Vice-Admiral E N Syfret
HMAS Nestor: Royal Australian Navy Destroyer
        Commander Alvord Rosenthal
HMS Nigeria: A Cruiser
SS Ohio: Eagle Shipping Company
        Captain Dudley W Mason,
        Chief Bosun's mate Charlie Walker
MV Orari: New Zealand Shipping company
HMS Pathfinder: A Destroyer
        Commander E A Gibbs
SS Pasteur: French passenger ship used as a troop ship –
known to the troops as 'Pasture'.
HMS Penn: Destroyer
HMS Phoebe: A cruiser
MV Port Chalmers: Commonwealth and Dominion Line
        Captain Henry G B Pinkney
HMS Primula: A corvette
Robust: A tug
MV Rochester Castle: Union-Castle Mail steamship Co
HMS Rodney: A Battleship
SS Santa Elisa: Grace Line
HMS Sirius: A cruiser
MV Sydney Star: Blue Star Line
        Carptain Thomas S Horn, Chief Engineer G Haig,
        Operation Substance
MV Troilus: Blue Funnel Line
HMS Victorious: An Aircraft carrier
MV Waimarama: Shaw Savill and Albion Co
        Cadet Fred Treves, Radio operator John Jackson,
        Lt Withers
MV Wairangi: Shaw, Savill and Albion Co
West Dene: A tug
HMS Wolverine: A Destroyer
        Lt Commander PW Gretton

To my grandfather, Jim Honeybill, 1903-1993
and my mother, Greta Davies, 1933 - 1992

Convoy

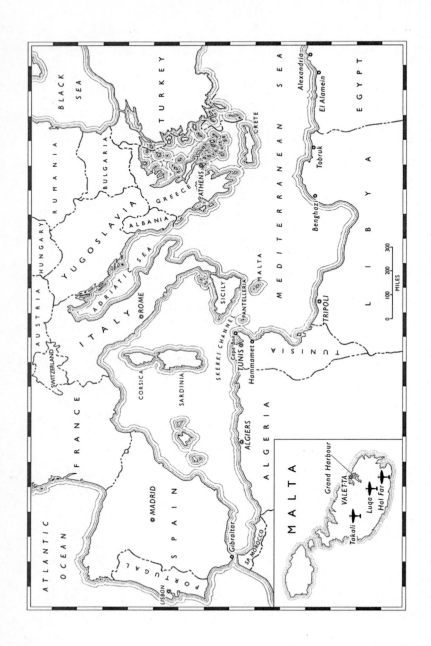

Sirens

When the sirens sound we huddle
under the kitchen table.
Mam, Nain and me.

It's oak, it will keep us safe
when the house falls down.
Nain says Liverpool's taking it bad.

The docks are on fire.
Here we see no planes,
but hear both sirens and stories

under the table. Nain tells
the tale of the lost orange,
how it fell from the tree.

My daddy has picked it up
and wrapped it in a white hanky,
safe in the pocket of his kitbag.

I try to remember having a father.
I have a photo of him and four
other sailors, smiling from the rails of a ship.

And postcards. His last one
full of sunshine.

No Medals?

Everything changes the day your ship
becomes a target, then turns into a trophy
in the hands of the enemy.

Weeks at sea turn into months.
As clenched and hard-bitten as the crew.

No softness now except in the eyes of the lads
becoming men before their time.

The ordinary, the able seamen,
just plying our trade.

Who will remember us?
Will there be medals for the likes of us?

Written on Board the Ajax

South Stack.
Three hundred and ninety-nine steps.
Wind spits soft rain.

The Blue Funnel Line,
two days out from Liverpool.
Four hours on. Four hours off.

Cape Town.
Pineapples and watermelons. Sent home
postcard of Table Mountain.

Bombay.
Coconuts and curry. Half the crew
down with dysentery.
Four on. Four off.

Coming back via Suez.
Malta. Sky dark with thunder.
Oil on the water.

Gibraltar: turning for home.
The Irish Sea – rain – a wet slap.
No light from South Stack.
Coastline for miles, dark.

Liverpool: Seventy-two hours in port.
No time to go home.

Packing Cases
Monday, 10 June, 1940: Declaration of war by Italy

350 bombers: Cants, Savoias, BR20s.
200 fighters: CR42s, Reggiane 2001s, Macchis.
First-class airfields sixty miles from Malta,
skilled pilots trained in Spain and Abyssinia.

Assessment of Maltese air defences.
Three airfields: Hal Far, Takali and Luqa,
none fully functioning.
Seaplane base at Kalafranc. No aircraft.

Chief Admin Officer's report:
Have located packing cases on slipway at Kalafranc
Marked H.M.S Glorious, Norway.
These contain component parts for naval Sea Gladiators.

Air Commodore Maynard
to Admiral Cunningham at Alexandria:
Request permission to unpack crates
and make use of your planes to defend island.

Granted with the most cordial approval.
Don't expect to get them back intact.

What odds – what fun.
Our few against five hundred and fifty.
Ours sturdy biplanes.
Theirs modern fighters.

We form a fighter flight of seven:
Squadron Leader Martin.
Flight Lieutenant Keeble (Pete).
Flying officers Hartley (Peter),
Waters (John), Woods (Timber).

Pilot officer Alexander (Peter),
and Flight Lieutenant Burgess
(George) – that's me.

Our planes can turn on a sixpence
can climb like a bat out of hell.
They have no vices at all.
More of the enemy than I can count
but we'll give them a good fight.

Formations of Savoias
approaching Valletta
at fifteen thousand feet.

We climb and climb
till we are above them.
Get in a good burst at 200 yards.

Fire returned. I break away.
Machine guns behind me.
Go into a steep left-hand turn.

The Macchi dives and fires.
We circle tightly
til I get him in my sights.

Full deflection: he goes down,
black smoke pours from his tail.
Straight into the sea at Grand Harbour.

Malta is no longer defenceless but
The Italian bombers are faster. So our only chance
is to scramble and climb quick as we can.
Hope to get four or five thousand feet
above them by the time they reach the island.
Then dive on them from the beam.

...

Bastards are throwing everything at us.
Massed formations, decoy planes
shadowed by packs of fighters.
Stragglers falling out of formation
to tempt us into a fight we can't win.

Over a hundred raids and we're still airborne
but not unscathed. Land with tail unit
dangling by a single strut.

My Glad's a colander with bullet holes.
Landing wheels shot off.
We struggle on.

I've enough St Christopher's
to keep me on the ground,
and the prayers of the Maltese.

Letter from Australia
24th June 1940

We've had a letter from Australia
from Doris M Roberts, shocked at the fall of France.
They're not family but they've looked after my dad
and uncle Bob whenever they're in Melbourne
providing a haven and somewhere to sleep ashore.

Now they want me to go and live with them
in the sunshine with a room of my own.
I've taken the letter to read myself
including all the bits Mam left out.
'We hear they are sending the children from England
in case of an invasion. If you would like us
to have Greta out here we would love
to look after her for you until the war is over.
I know it would be terrible to part with her.'

Mam says I can't go,
says it's too dangerous,
says the Germans will sink anything
says something about the Lusitania.

I ask her if my dad's ship has been sunk.
She tells me not to be so stupid.
Said there'd have been a telegram
like the family at the Refail
when their boy was lost over the English Channel.
Says *You're not going to Australia
and that's final*.

I would still like to go to Australia.
They have koala bears you can cuddle.
Mine has lost his claws.

Faith, Hope and Charity

Someone suggests names –
Pip, Squeak and Wilfred –
but John says
Faith, Hope and Charity.

The Maltese believe
we're shooting down enemy
planes, left, right and centre.
We're not but does it matter?

France has surrendered.
We will be fighting on Malta's beaches
before we know it.

We've been at it for weeks
and then we lose Pete Keeble.

He shakes one off
but the other is on his tail
and follows him down.

Pete goes under the wireless aerials,
a desperate stunt, and it doesn't work.
The Italian crashes in the same field.

I'm flying punch-drunk, weaving about the sky.
We lose another plane but her pilot bales out.

We're at Hal Far waiting to be scrambled
when we hear fighters approach.
AA guns surprisingly silent.
We look up: monoplanes.
My God, they're Hurricanes.

Operation White, November 1940

The range of a Hurricane MK II (tropicalized) in still air, at 130 knots, at 10,000 feet is 521 miles.

– Pilot's Handling Notes

We need more planes.
We're defending the island with only
one Gladiator, four Hurricanes.
REPEAT. WE NEED MORE PLANES.

'Operation White to proceed. Admiral Somerville to escort Argus and her Hurricanes to within flying distance of Malta; aircraft to take off in two sub flights of six, each led by a Fleet Air Arm Skua (with observer to plot best course for the island). Air Officer Commanding Malta to have two Sunderlands waiting over the island to escort the Hurricanes for the final stage.'

Subflight 1: Flying Officer J.A.F. Maclachlan, DFC

Speed 150 mph, height 2,000 feet

Am dropping smoke floats.
The wind has changed. Dead ahead –
will be hard pressed to reach Malta
before we run out of fuel.

Sea mist thick,
a patchwork of fog and cloud.
I'm flying blind.

Forty-five miles short of Malta
I hear the engine of another Hurricane
cut. Stone silent.

She spirals into the sea.
I break formation and follow.
The pilot floats, a dark blob
amongst the waves.
I call up the Sunderland and fly

low over the pilot, rocking my wings,
until the Sunderland on the sea
hauls him aboard.

Four Hurricanes ahead
following the single Skua.
A veil of cloud:
only three come out.

Two minutes later,
Luqa's dusty runway.
We plummet, manage to land.
There's not enough fuel left in my tank
to cover an upended sixpence.

Subflight 2

'A tragic loss of vitally needed planes'

No sign of the island.
No welcoming Sunderland.

SHEPHERD 2. SHEPHERD 2.
Where are you?

Bill's War Diary

Sergeant William Lazell, Royal Artillery

Arrived at Gourock in Scotland
Embarked on T.M.S. Pasture
Now out at sea.

Wonder what is in store for us?
Wrote letters home. Food good
but not getting any sleep.

Dive-bombers, torpedoes, e-boats,
had quite a warm time.
Shot down five planes.

Arrived at Malta.
All quiet during day.
Air raids at night.

Sent airmail home.
Think I shall like Malta
in spite of the flies.

Few bombs during night.
Waiting for my full pay.
Army owes me 9/6.

First action.
Got three enemy planes,
saw two of them crash in flames.

Canteen had some Cadburys
nut milk chocolate.
Tasted lovely.

...

Another quiet day.
Must have scared
the Wops away.

Bored stiff.
Wish Jerry would come back
and give us some fun.

Fired up two Wops.
Congratulated on accurate firing.
Command seem to appreciate our work.

Very hot raid.
Sticks of bombs across the site.
Two sergeants injured.

Our best pilots have gone
to Russia. Whole day of raids.
Four letters arrived.

Taken three months to get here.
My first birthday away from home.
I'm twenty one years old

Sydney Star – Operation Substance
Captain Thomas Sydney Horn

She's a beauty, my *Sydney Star*, my namesake,
built by Harland and Wolff:
they know how to turn out a fine ship.

She was launched for Blue Star five years ago.
Became mine on her maiden voyage. It's just her and me now.
I won't be bothering with another wife.

She's fast: Liverpool to Australia in less than five weeks.
We've enjoyed honeymoon times
but this will be different.

Saturday July 12th 1941

We're awaiting our orders,
alongside the *City of Pretoria,*
as the sky clouds with mist and rain.

We're joined by *Port Chalmers,*
a Blue Flue ship *Deucalion,*
the destroyer *Jacob Van Heemskerck.*
Everyone waiting
for someone else to decide what to do.

Never been convoy commodore.
I tell 'em: *Form a column*
at three cables on Sydney Star.
To my great surprise they fall
in line as we head south.

Here comes the heavy mob.
The Admiral's battleship, *HMS Nelson*
Cruisers: *Arethusa, Edinburgh* and *Manchester.*
More merchantmen – *Melbourne Star, Avila Star*
Pasteur, Durham

and an Irish Sea Ferry *Leinster*.
We're in the hands of the Navy. Their game now.
We're still heading south towards warmer waters.
If we're damaged, my crew will stand half a chance.

We're carrying the 32nd Light AA regiment.
Twenty officers and four hundred and forty six men.
Off to Malta or Egypt I reckon.

Sunday July 20th 1941

Our orders fired by rocket line
from *HMAS Nestor* as she comes alongside.
A sealed packet to be opened at noon.

From Admiral Somerville:

For over twelve months Malta has resisted all assaults of the enemy. The gallantry displayed by the garrison and people of Malta has aroused admiration throughout the world. To enable their defence to be continued, it is essential that your ships with their valuable cargoes, should arrive safely in Grand Harbour. The Royal Navy will escort and assist you in this great mission; you on your part can assist the Royal Navy by giving strict attention to the following points:
Don't make smoke.
Don't show any lights at night.
Keep good station.
Don't straggle.
If your ship is damaged, keep her going at the best possible speed.
Provided every officer and man realizes that it is up to him to do his duty to the very best of his ability I feel sure we shall succeed.
Remember that the signal is THE CONVOY MUST GO THROUGH.

We're in fog off Gib.
So Axis spies on the Rock
won't see the convoy slipping past.

I'm as old as this century.
Tonight I feel each year like an anchor's weight.
Visibility down to next to nothing.
My look-outs strain into thick white mist,

their pupils dilated in the dark.
Ahead of us the *Melbourne Star*.
Don't show any lights at night.
we were ordered,
but we can hardly see her –
just a faint plume
of water from her fog buoy.
Let's hope *Deucalion* following behind
will be able to keep to her place in the line.

Leinster's run aground.
We light our navigation lights.
And douse them when the fog clears at dawn.
With great relief we increase our speed
to close formation.

Edinburgh makes to *Port Chalmers*.
You were a long way astern
even before the fog came down.
S stands for Straggler. And also for Sunk.

Tuesday July 22nd 1941

Heading east. Sea calm.
Wind north-easterly and light. Sky cloudless.
We're hugging the Moroccan coastline.
Fulmars from *Ark Royal* on patrol.
No sign of the enemy.

Wednesday July 23rd 1941

We're screened by destroyers, moving like a blunt-nosed arrow.
With us 'til we enter the Skerki channel

17:15
Nelson, Renown, Ark Royal turn back.
Feel defenceless without them
but I know all about the fate of the *Illustrious*.

I could do with a kip.
Have not left the bridge since we sailed.
I should lie down on the chart room settee but I don't.

Thursday July 24th 1941

We're creeping past Pantelleria,
through the enemy's minefields,
an approach he's not likely to suspect.

02:50
Cossack and *Edinburgh* open fire with Bofors, Oerlikons.
Searchlights white and dazzling
blaze out of the darkness so I'm blinded.

I cover my eyes with my hands
and then open my fingers to let in the light.
Oh Christ.

MAS-boats in our midst
moving faster than I can keep track of them.
The wake of a torpedo coming straight for us, fifty yards to port.

03:05
We must change course.
I start to shout the order into the telephone tube
and we're hit
amidships. My namesake shudders.

A pillar of flame
rises high as her funnel
and then just as suddenly it goes out.

As her deck shifts beneath my boots,
I'm aware of the ingress of water
that pours through her shattered hull.

I feel like I've been punched as well as her,
but I must save the troops.
Quietly I give the order - abandon ship stations.

They're mustered at the lifeboats
when my crew tell me
they're unusable, damaged
in the earlier shell-fire.

I signal *Nestor:*
Request immediate assistance
to disembark troops.

Commander Alvord Rosenthal of *Nestor* to *Sydney Star:*
Why are you so far astern?
You appear undamaged.

Captain Thomas. S. Horn of *Sydney Star* to *Nestor*
Have been torpedo'd in No. 3 hold.
Water levels rising.
REPEAT Request assistance.

Nestor to *Sydney Star:*
Coming alongside.
Make ready.
We're only a few miles from Pantelleria
I can hear engines.
The enemy searching for us in the dark.

My crew work in silence
rigging planks, cargo ladders
to Nestor's fo'csle.

No need to tell them to hurry. In fifty minutes
they get every man off.

Thursday July 24th 1941

03:30
First mate hands me Haig's damage report
Water rising in three forward holds.
Pumps not helping. Can give you twelve knots.

Horn to Rosenthal:
I'm staying.
We're not finished yet.

I decide to set course direct for Malta
We'll ship water whatever our speed.
Daylight in an hour.

We have to get clear of the enemy's base.
Course 116 degrees, speed 12 knots
Have hopes we'll make it.

Sunrise. An empty sea.
No. 1 hold 12 feet of water.
No. 2 7 feet. No. 3 33 feet.
Rest of ship dry.

Two Italian Savoias
circle like storm crows
just out of range.

My ship has guns.
A high angle 3-inch gun,
four Bofors and three machine guns.

But we have no gun crews.
They are all on the *Nestor*.
I call for volunteers.

The oilers and greasers
dirt-faced but eager
throw themselves at our guns.

The Savoias met by an unholy barrage
of curses and gunfire from our Bofors,
drop their torpedoes at some distance.

Take violent evasive action,
As does *Nestor*.
We come through unscathed.

The carpenter brings me soundings
that make the hairs on my neck go stiff,
but I thank him and what I write is:
Water continues to rise
in holds 1, 2 and 3.
We reduce speed to 9 knots.

Thursday July 24th 1941

07:00
Another lone Savoia so close
its torpedo explodes
in our wake.

07:32
Nestor fires at everything
that moves in the sky
and much that doesn't.

08:00
Destroyer *Hermione*
races back from the convoy
to take up station by our side.

My ship settles lower by the head.
Lists to port. Steering difficult.
She fights me as she flounders.

I signal *Nestor*
Pumps no longer holding.

Swinging badly.
Sorry.
Al Rosenthal to Tom Horn
Would a reduction in speed help?

I don't think so. Not at the moment

Al Rosenthal
Would hate to lose you now.
Am considering alternative sites
for beaching if flooding
progresses to dangerous levels.

I send him details,
cargo stowage arrangements.
Malta only twenty miles distant.
Have hopes we'll make it.

Thursday July 24th 1941

10:00
More Savoias out of the sun.
Ju 87s from the opposite
direction. I try to swing her head on.

She wallows. Refuses to turn.
One Savoia passes between our masts.
Another tilts to clear our stern.

She's laden with water.
Must have taken in close
to her own displacement.

Eleven days on this bridge.
I've had no sleep since Monday.
Am I risking my crew?

If the bulkheads fail
she'll go down within minutes.
But the watchword is

THE CONVOY MUST GO THROUGH.

More bombers. Quite unable
to take avoiding action.
Fortunately a near miss but lots of splinters.

Sudden silence with the attack over.
My ship is sinking. She's settling by the head
and listing to a dangerous extent.

We've stopped the engines.
Eighteen miles to Malta.
I must not lose her.

I give the order to restart engines.
If we don't work up more speed
she'll flounder before we reach the harbour.

My hand tightens on the engine-room telegraph
In one even pull surprisingly steady
I take her to 'full ahead'.

14:40
Pilot boarded off breakwater; helm and engines as requisite for
approaching harbour.

14:41
Tug *Robust* fast for'ard port bow.

14:51
Tug *Ancient* fast amidships, starboard side. Tug *West Dene*
assisting where necessary.

16:00
Vessel securely moored fore and aft.

A sound from the breakwater,
like distant waves on the shore,
I realise this is people cheering.

Seems I'm some kind of hero
- in line for a medal
but the message I treasure most.

'The Royal Navy offer you their congratulations on a very fine
piece of seamanship.'

My ship has a breach in her side,
which should have made an end of her,
but we've survived, both me and her.

Under Fire

After the salvo of shells,
you can no longer hear.

Young Taff Williams is hunched,
his mouth an open wound.

You move towards him with legs
like a deep sea diver's.

Step over ruptures
in the deck plates. The fires

bloom black smoke. Williams' face
is a mask of blood.

As you hoist him onto your shoulder
you notice for the first time how

your jacket's blown off,
your shirt's in tatters;

how Williams clutches
your hand like a baby.

Going Down

We've said prayers for Williams and the others.
The sea, stilled as if listening.
The sky's an irrational blue.

We weighted the shrouds with spent shell cases
so they'll go straight down.

I try to remember his laugh, his love of words.
Nothing but his mouth
wide-open in a scream.

I should write to his mother,
to tell her he died without pain.

Unprotected Water

We've reached what they call Grand Harbour.
I hope Birkenhead looks better.
Here there's little left standing.

I'm called upon to row the Captain
ashore and make haste,
glad to escape the chore of unloading.

We're deep in unprotected water
when the air fills with their bombers.
The whole sky trembles;

Jerry come to finish off our convoy.
And we're in our open boat
as the water churns around us.

I ship the oars as I duck.
His hand grasps my arm. *If we're hit*
you won't feel a thing. Now keep rowing.

Ashamed, I put my strength
into moving the ruddy boat. Moor up.
Well done, he says under his breath.

Unloading

The Maltese are thin as ghosts before their time.
And grateful. I've never before been kissed
on both cheeks by a grown man.
Thank you, thank you, he said, crying.

Some of our crew say they ate rats
in the caves, before we arrived.

Now I understand our orders
as we left England.

Remember the watchword –
the convoy must go through.

Overseas Posting

I pretend they've got a sudden posting
overseas. We're abroad already
but they've gone on ahead.

To Egypt probably, harrying Rommel's army.
The fact they took off with us but didn't land
can be ignored.

They're in another officers' mess
somewhere. Still cracking jokes.
Phelps with his pipe.

His wife back in Blighty
with a baby on the way. I tell myself
he's there with her,

getting ready to lean over the cradle.
The baby will have his blue eyes
and lop-sided way of smiling.

So I never write the letter to tell her
I'm sorry he's bought it.

Don't...

Based on the account of Tom Neil, DFC, AFC, AE, 249 Squadron

It's eighth November 1941 and you're off duty.
Today it's the turn of 126 Squadron.
Leaving the officers' mess you walk up to dispersal.

The sky holds splattered smudges of ack-ack.
Hurricanes circle the airfield.
After last summer's battle you always count them back.

One Hurricane stutters:
bullet holes, gun patches gone,
You sprint towards her as she lands.
Her propeller turns.
Her pilot slumps, still masked.
'Are you all right?'
They got me in the back.

It's Pat Lardner-Burke.
No winch, no crane, no help.
'Pat. I can't get at you. You have to stand.'
He groans but hauls his body upright with shaking hands.
You grasp his shoulders; Pat's face against
your chest. A grotesque embrace.

As you begin to lift him, Pat croaks an entreaty
Christ, Ginger. Please.
For Christ's sake don't shake me.

That Bullet

Once Lardner-Burke has been taken to hospital
I gather the others and we go to his Hurricane –
clod-hopping carthorse of a machine.
She's been hit by point-fives from a Macchi 202.

Instead of the usual metal work dimples
that the Germans inflict – holes gape like black mouths.
Punched through the armour-plate as if it were tin foil.

The bullet went through the back of the seat
hit Pat in the chest and disappeared
into the darkness below the dashboard.
I think of how he clung to me and I don't look for it.

I see your ships

Your mother takes you down to the harbour
where you can see the merchant ships.
She recites their names; *Ajax, Clan Fergusson,
Sydney Star, City of Calcutta* like a litany.

All the island cheered from these rooftops
in the summer when the ships came in.
Now you can no longer see the hole
in Sydney Star's side left by the torpedo.

They say she should have sunk
but her crew kept pumping.
Now her captain is down in the harbour
making ready to take her back to sea.

The cranes rumble, and your stomach
grumbles in sympathy.
It's been a poor Christmas. You can't
remember not being hungry.

You're counting down to your coming of age.
You still can't decide, Air Force or Army?
Today you'll make up your mind.
It has to be the merchant navy.

Christmas 1941

After three months of dodging the bombing
the *Ajax* is moored upstream
at the head of Marsa creek.

The bombs still come every day.
Her crew take shelter in the caves.
One watch on board.

She's hit on Christmas Eve.
The bomb passes clean through her bow.
No explosion. Just bubbles of water.

The Chinese greaser first back on board.
No matter how hard he searches
he can't find what he seeks.

No sign of the crate. Not a single feather.
A lingering rank chicken smell from the corner
where they'd been fed. Given water.

A hole in the ship's side instead of
the New Year's dinner. He takes it personally,
this intervention of the Luftwaffe.

On their unmarried mothers, sons and daughters
he calls down curses. Until this moment
he hadn't fully seen the point of the war.

Death's Door

Based on the account of Raoul Daddo-Langlois, 249 Squadron

Grounded: no planes fit to fly.
Spend day building blast pens.
Never knew sand-bags could be this heavy.

Mid-afternoon their bombers come over;
in a rush we take shelter in a slit trench.
Air chokes with dust.

After the raid we scramble out
and start clearing debris.
Two 109s fill the horizon
spitting machine gun bullets.
We fling ourselves down,
get arms and legs into the trench.

Then they are gone
and all of us safe
but how I shake. The others also.
At least in the air I can shoot back. Here
you just sit it out.

Sign of the Cross

Based on the account of Squadron Leader P B 'Laddie' Lucas, 249 Squadron

This island's all limestone
rough, arid, rock-strewn.
Nowhere to force land.

Smoke from the engine thickens the cockpit –
I should step out into a limitless sky.
Fear clenches its fist at the back of my neck.

At a thousand feet a green glimpse
 – a small field
beyond miles of limestone.

Wheels up, flaps down,
I slow almost to a stall,
hold her into the wind.

My Spit settles into soft earth, engine smoking,
a few yards short of a blunt stone wall.
I scramble clear.

Three Maltese women in long black dresses
stumble over rough ground.
Each clutches a hessian sack filled with soil
for the burning engine.

I signal them away
with my hands like an explosion.
They step back, shake their heads.

The oldest, to judge from the lines on her face,
walks slowly to the Spitfire.
She pats its wing and comes back towards me.

Gentle, she touches my forearm,
makes the sign of the cross, smiles.

Another of us

We shouldn't have let him fly,
still half asleep after a night in Valletta
What was the woman's name?
I never found out.

Sweet she was, he said:
she helped him forget.
A few hours' respite.
We could all do with that.

We shouldn't have let him fly.
After the melée,
once the 109s had buggered off
I heard him asking where we were.

He was way down below us
at Angels 8, we were at 15
I'll come up he said.
I saw a 109 coming in fast.

Break Dougie, break.

I shouldn't have let him fly;
I should have stopped him.
I saw him bale out,
White silk canopy floating down.
Bastard 109 makes another run.
White circle collapsing
under the force of its slipstream.

Turn away

In the future, after this war, when the name of Malta is mentioned, you will be able to say with pride 'I was there'.

Air-Vice Marshall Hugh Pughe Lloyd, AOC Malta

We're sleeping in tents
on account of the lack
of accommodation at Takali.

We're among the olive trees:
gnarled trunks with leaves
that turn silver.

At least the officer's mess is still standing,
and the Group Captain gave us a good speech.

Woken by the crackle of cannon fire. Me109s
strafing Takali.
The raid over, we walk
in sunshine to the mess for a frugal breakfast.

A Hurricane pouring smoke at eight hundred feet.
Her pilot climbs from the cockpit.

His parachute streams flat
behind him – totally useless
as he falls.

Airfields
Air Marshall Sir Hugh Pughe Lloyd, AOC Malta

The enemy has changed his tactics.
Having failed to defeat us in the air,
our airfields are now his target.

Five-hundred pound bombs,
one thousand pound bombs, incendiary bombs,
delayed action bombs, bombs linked by chains
that tumble like skittles.

Am depending on the Army
to make good the damage.
West Kents and Royal Artillery to Luqa.
Dorsets and Buffs to Hal Far.
Manchesters and Inniskillings to Takali.

An attack on Takali by eighty Junkers this evening.
I take Woodhall and Satchell to see the worst.
It is very dark. There are mounds of earth
and men at work with buckets and spades
as the island does not have a bulldozer.

We become separated among the craters,
and shout – each fearing
the other is stranded without help,
until we find each other by voice alone.
Takali will be out for a week I decide.

The next afternoon I'm told Takali
is back in service. From the air
it must look like a Somme battlefield.
I feel a moment of quiet satisfaction
that we can still fly
despite what the enemy's photo reconnaissance
must be showing him.

Hope for the Hungry

There are no more eggs
since they ate the chickens.
The shelves are barren of food.

Grandmother sings as she hangs
washing out to dry. Her rough hands
veined with blue.
Songs of men who go to war
and never return.

The boy listens from the back step,
his dark head turned
listening to the stories.
No school today because of the air-raids.

But grandmother will insist
on maths once the washing's out.
If he's obedient she might
have a search through the cupboards.
Find him a morsel to eat.

Pink, then Scarlet

I'm going to Myfanwy's party on Saturday.
She will be ten. Her house is big enough
for all the children to fit in.

Nain has washed our best dress.
It hung on the line for three days
before it dried.

The invitation is pink,
like my dress. Not everyone has one.
Nain says I'll look like a cherry blossom.

Nobody will know the dress
belonged to her. Nain says,
this is our secret.

I feel sick. My school blouse
is too tight. My neck
itches–red rash where I've scratched.

The dress will be pretty.
Myfanwy will be my friend forever and ever
and my father will come home.

The pink dress hangs in the wardrobe.
The doctor's dark-haired–serious. He holds
a stethoscope to my chest.

He says he's sorry
I'm the third case he's seen.
I have to stay indoors for a week.

Nain says *Why isn't he fighting Hitler?*
He should be ashamed.
Miserable coward.

Operation Vigorous: June 1942

Are we sailing to our deaths again?
I'm sick of this, these runs to Malta
Not supposed to admit it.

When the sky fills up with their bombers
I get the shakes. Just my knees, mind,
nothing else.

My hands quite steady so no one can tell
except the old man, who seems to know
I'm not made of flint – not like the others.

Dreamt last night I was home.
The house had caught fire,
smoke belched from the roof.

Me and Maggie in the back yard
when we realise the little 'un
is still inside, up in her bedroom.

She turned nine last month
but I remember her as small enough
to carry on your shoulders.

I pelted back into the house.
Maggie calling after me to be quick.
Up the stairs three at a time.

She was tucked in a white sheet,
thumb in her mouth.
Brown wavy hair across the pillow.

Flames licked round the window.
Brought out sweat all over my body.

Picked her up, still wrapped in the sheet.
Had to stamp out the fire advancing across the floor.

If we're hit, you won't feel a thing.
I tell myself again though I don't believe it.

Would like to hear him say
Well done one more time.

My child over my shoulder
like a little sack of potatoes
when she turns into Williams.

Clutches at my hand, gasping
like there's no air left to breathe.
Still haven't written to his mother.

I promise I'll do it
when we get back to Alexandria.
If I'm spared.

Message from the Governor of Malta – April 1942
*I can only speak for Malta itself and our situation is so grave that it is
my duty to restate it in the clearest possible terms…When the question
of running a convoy from Egypt in March was under consideration I
said the problem of maintaining the Fortress had reached a critical point.
It has now gone beyond that point and it is obvious that the very worst
will happen if we cannot replenish our vital needs especially flour and
ammunition and that very soon. … If Malta is to be held, drastic action
is needed now it is a question of survival.*

At Haifa we're assigned
Lieutenant Aylwin as our liaison
– keeps asking how we know our destination.

It's supposed to be secret.
Who's he trying to kid.
Once you're loaded

with grain, petrol, ammunition
and coal you know it's a run
to Malta. Nothing need be said.

Nonetheless he goes off muttering
about careless talk and how
we'll pay. Won't tell him

about the crates I took in
labelled 'Wembley Stores – Malta'.
He'll do his nut.

It's nearly dark when the telephone rings
Ops no doubt to tell us to stand down.
We've been flying all day. Instead it's Woodhall.

There are twelve plus bombers
flying from Sicily towards the ships.
No fighters. I know it's late

and will mean night landings
but we'd like you to send four aircraft.
Convoy's been taking a pounding.

We'd like to give them this support.
I'll go sir, with Jones, Linton, Watts.
They're all clued up.

Once airborne Woody gives us
variations in vector. *They're below*
you – should see them soon now.

We drop a couple of thousand feet
to provide extra speed.
About a dozen 88s – sharp etched

against the setting sun.
Flying straight and level
in tight boxes of four.

They haven't seen us
coming up from below
against the darkening sea.

It's classic textbook stuff.
Too late when they spot
the flashes from our cannon.

Every man for himself
as they break all over the sky
firing back.

They must think we're a couple
of squadrons at least.
Like shooting duck as twilight turns into night.

Dark specks against the fading sky
and I'm a small boy
with my father, before the war.

Laddie Lucas

'Bomb alley' they call this.
I've lost track of how long
we've been under attack.

If it weren't for the old man,
John Scott, we'd be at the bottom
of the ocean.

His trick is to watch astern
as the bomber lines up.
Then order helm hard over

Stop one engine so she swings.
Near miss every time.
Doesn't half make you jump

what with the geysers
of water and the *Ajax* shudders.
Feel sick but stay at my post.

ADM 199/1244 Lt P Aylwin
I cannot speak too highly of the master, Captain J.R. Scott, a man of 40
years' sea service and 60 years of age. He remained calm throughout and
accepted without hesitation any advice I had to give, for taking avoiding
action during air attacks.

Most of the ships
that started with us
have gone back.

Aagtekirk and *Primula*
both with engine problems
off to Tobruk.

Bhutan's been sunk.
It's dark now.
Should mean a lull.

The enemy keeps dropping flares.
Exposed –
like being caught without your clothes.

They say the Italian fleet's
on its way out
to finish us off.

Photo reconnaissance report of situation at Taranto.
Battleships *Littorio* and *Vittorio Veneto* and four cruisers at sea.

Message from the Rear Admiral Vian to Admiral Harwood:
Do you wish me to retire? With good weather expected tomorrow
we can't hold off the Italians. We are down to a third of our
ammunition.

From Harwood to Vian:
Suggest you proceed westwards and turn back at 02:00

Vian:
I wish he'd be more decisive.
Really quite a difficult situation.

We shall do our best.
Have been torpedoed before
when the *Naiad* was sunk - survived.

Perhaps our air strikes
against the Italian battle fleet
might succeed.

From Harwood to Vian:
I must leave the decision to you whether to comply with my previous order, or whether to again retire with the hope of carrying out a night destroyer attack, if the enemy stands on.

We've been told it's a victory
of sorts. The enemy's losses
include a damaged battleship.

Troilus and *Orari* made it to Malta.
But we're back in Alex.
A paper copy of the Admiral's message

makes me feel brave for a minute.
I lift it by the corners
prise it off the wall. Stuff it into my pocket.

Our convoy has been turned back and under a heavy and sustained state of attack we have suffered losses.

As to the first the enemy interposed his main fleet between our convoy and MALTA but in so doing left himself with insufficient force to prevent some ships reaching the island from westwards.

As to the second this was not one-sided, not withstanding his geographical and numerical advantage his losses include an eight inch cruiser and a destroyer sunk and several ships damaged including a battleship.

A Letter from My Daddy

'Tonight we saw dolphins following
in the wake of the ship.
There were six, splashing in the foam.
'A school' is what I think
a group of dolphins is called.

Your Mam tells me you are doing well
at school and set to skip
a year ahead. I hope you will continue
to work hard and have prizes
to show me when I get home.'

Glimmer of Light

10th August 1942 126 Squadron

Pilot officer Jerrold Smith flying with a sergeant pilot
standing in as wingman for his brother, Roderick.

Jerry who was always top of his class
who was only a year older
who always carried an electric torch.

There are reports of a parachute descending
east of Grand Harbour.
It's dusk but Rod asks his flight commander
for permission to search the eastern approaches.
Going over and over the darkening sea
in the hunt for a glimmer of light.

Memorial Occasion

Pilot Officer Rod Smith

I followed the practice
I always adopted on memorial occasions.
I put into neutral that part of my brain
which ponders such matters
and carried on quietly.

Operation Pedestal: 8-15 August, 1942

The Royal Navy trained for war; war caught the merchant marine going about its everyday business.

– Malta Convoys, Richard Woodman

Lieutenant Commander Roger Hill, HMS Ledbury

Pedestal: the last all-out attempt
to get a convoy through. No aviation fuel,
no submarine diesel. Food running out.
Malta virtually at a standstill.

Our convoy of over fifty ships left Gibraltar
with thirteen merchantmen and the tanker, *Ohio*,
steaming in four columns.
All big fast ships doing fifteen knots.

Close round the convoy a screen of anti-aircraft destroyers
including my *Ledbury*.
Battleships *Nelson* and *Rodney* astern.
Cruiser *Cairo* with a roving commission.

Inside the destroyer screen, three aircraft carriers:
Victorious, Indomitable, Eagle.
They carry a total of seventy-two fighters.
Cruisers *Sirius, Phoebe, Charybis*
keep guard on the carriers.

Finally, old *Furious* with her own destroyer screen
carries 38 Spitfires
to be flown five hundred miles to Malta.

Crete and Greece in German hands.
The toe of Italy, Sardinia, Sicily
all aerodromes.
20 submarines, 40 E-boats.
We're entering their cauldron of attack;
it'll be another charge of the Light Brigade.
My job is to stay by the merchant ships.

I have promised my crew we will remain with them
regardless. Never again let it be said
the Royal Navy ran away.

I remember PQ17 every day,
those signals coming through at midnight
on the Merchant Navy channel
and passed to me on the bridge.

Am being bombed by large numbers of planes.
On fire in the ice.
Six U-boats approaching on surface.
Abandoning ship.
We left twenty-three to their fate.

This time it begins on August 11th:
an attack by high-level bombers.
We have a steady shoot at them.
I hear the carrier fighter control officer
calmly instruct the pilots.

Our favourite pilot, our friend Red Leader:
Large number of bandits below me to port – attacking,
I say again, attacking.
They chase away the Ju 88s.

Not all of ours land successfully.
Those that crash and burst into flames
have to be swept over the side
to keep the carrier clear. Poor sods.

Before dawn on August 12th we hear our fighters
taking off. The enemy attacks at 0915
sweeping through the convoy.

Never seen bombs in the air before.
One drops into the sea so close
it soaks the gun crew.
Rather frightening.

We listen as Red Leader goes after more 'bandits'.
We listen as his control calls: *Red Leader, Red Leader*.
Another voice: *Red Leader has been shot down*.

We see a parachute and go
to pluck him from the water. But I have a sudden doubt,
lean over, call out to my first lieutenant, *What is he, Jimmy?*

A fucking Hun sir.
Three more parachutes come down;
let them go to hell.

Able Seaman, Blue Funnel Line

They tell me that aviation fuel floats.
Floats, and burns on the sea's surface.
Your only hope is to keep clear.

But I can't swim. Burn or drown,
I don't fancy either.

I can man a gun. Done my training.
Anything that comes near us,
we'll shoot it down.

Roger Hill

It's 0430, in my chair on the bridge
with a hot cup of cocoa,
after two hours' uneasy sleep.

I allow my mind to entertain
brief worries about my Sub.
He was in a cruiser off Crete.

Bombed till they ran out of ammunition.
Then they had to take it
until they were sunk.

Not sure how he'll stand up
to any more bombing.
But he's reliable; let's hope he'll come through.

Able Seaman, Blue Star Line

My mate says to me,
Know what day it is tomorrow, do you?

August 11th, I says.

Yes but what day is it?

Tuesday?

*What do posh people do
on the 11th of August?*

I dunno, go on holiday?
a Mediterranean cruise?

*Nah – it's the start of the shooting season.
Only this year, we're the grouse.*

It's not funny but he laughs and laughs.

Geoffrey Wellum, pilot, HMS Furious

Sir, why are the armourers
taking the ammo out of my Spitfire?
Looks like cigarettes they're putting in?

*That's right.
Someone was worried about weight
preventing us taking off.*

Fags don't weigh much I suppose.

Indeed. Malta is short of smokes
as well as everything else.
It'll do morale a power of good.

That's kind of us, Sir.
I hope the Germans
and Italians don't know.

What if they do? You couldn't hit them
even if you had ammunition.

I would like to be able to try, Sir.

Flight deck officer, HMS Furious

Just the third flight to get off.
Nine of 'em to go.
Flight commander makes his final checks.

What was that rumble? Like a clap of thunder.
The *Eagle*: she's listing to port
billowing smoke. A torpedo?

Planes slide from her decks
vanish into the waves.
She can't be going down. Our sister ship.

She looks like a great grey slab
of a thing on her side like that.
I must not look.

Concentrate. Got to get this lot off.
Quick. Now. 35 knots of wind over the deck
to give them lift.

Raise both arms above my head.
In my right a green flag.
Thumbs up with my left.
Pilot gives me a quick nod.
I rotate my flag and they're off.

Bridge on HMS Furious

Keep clear, keep clear of carrier,
Air attack.
Wouldn't want to shoot you down.

Henry Rathbone, Visual Signals Rating, HMS Eagle

After many air raid alerts in the forenoon
I go down to the mess deck
hoping for a nap in my hammock

when we're hit.
A lunge, a plunge into dark
as she rolls.

Emergency lighting flicks on. I scramble
up the ladder to the main mess deck.
Use the tables as hand-holds

to climb towards the starboard ladder
a platform sticks out from the ship's side.
If only I can reach it.

My lifebelt's in good condition. I can swim.
Poor *Eagle* is practically on her side.
I walk into the sea and start to paddle.

The flight deck commander swims beside me
complete with gold braid. We exchange brief greetings,
Both of us intent on getting clear before she sinks.

Gracious old lady, her end peaceful.
No great suction to pull us down.

Destroyers drop depth charges. Hope they will stay
away from us. That awful thump
in the stomach after each explosion.

Am picked up by the tug, *Jaunty*.
Dozens of us. Find a large blue flag
in her signal locker, and dry myself with it.

Lt-Commander Gretton, HMS Wolverine

The little tug, *Jaunty* was an astonishing sight.
With so many men on board – some even up the rigging.
You couldn't see her for the mass of bodies.

Flag Officer, North Atlantic from Gibraltar to Vice Admiral Syfret

Warning - dusk air attack.
Expect large formation of enemy aircraft.

Admiral Syret

Hoist Q Flag
– all ships to be ready
for attack in seven minutes.

Fleet Air Arm Pilot

As we return to the convoy,
the light slow dying.
Ships no more than sketched patterns
on the grey steel plate of the sea.
We left them sailing peaceably
through the sunset.

Now in the dark
they're enclosed in a sparkling net
of tracers and bursting shells.
Every gun in the fleet fires.
Darkening air laced with threads
– beads of flame.

As we circle
bursts of fire follow us.
They're firing at anything that flies.
Where can we land?

Another pilot breaks radio silence,
I've got no fuel, I've got no fuel.
He makes for *Victorious* as she turns full helm.

His tank empty
but it still explodes
as he hits her deck.
An orange flash in the deepening dusk.

I dredge up reserves of courage,
from some forgotten fuel tank,
as I prepare to approach
through the barrage.

Suddenly I see *Indomitable*
All her deck lights shining,
leaving the screen of destroyers,
steaming a dead straight course.
Captain Thomas Troubridge giving us
a safe place to land.

Vice Admiral Syfret

The merchantmen have been drilled,
since we left Gibraltar,
 in making emergency turns,
altering speed and formation.

They have attained an efficiency
in manoeuvring
comparable to that of a fleet unit.

One can't help but feel
they are going to need it.

We can expect the waves of attacks to intensify.
This will be the most vital day
– the severest test of our skill.

Captain 'Eddie' Baines, Destroyer Bramham

Bombing starts in a big way on Wednesday August 12th.
Deucalion's near missed twice, then hit amidships.
She comes to a halt because she's making water.
Bramham being a rescue ship we come alongside.

We're greeted by the sight of *Deucalion's* boats
being lowered in a great panic and rowed towards us.
Her captain, Ramsey Brown, apoplectic on the bridge
shouts to us to send them back.

When they reach our scrambling nets
we stamp on their hands.
Tell them to return to the *Deucalion*.
They call us some choice names but they go back.

Captain Ramsey Brown, Master, Deucalion

Some greasers and assistant stewards took it upon themselves,
to lower numbers three and six lifeboats.
Not my regular crew.
They're drawn from the Merchant Navy pool.

Am going to reach Valletta come what may.
Engine room tell me we can make eight knots.
Shall attempt the inshore route
through the Tunisian narrows in the hope
of being undetected.

Eddie Baines

Because of *Deucalion's* slow speed
we're to escort her along the coast of North Africa.
As unpleasant a route as anywhere else.

At dusk a couple of bombers
arrive out of the murk. Pop a torpedo into *Deucalion*
Blow a bloody great hole in her stern.

She's full of aviation fuel.
This explodes.
We take on board her crew.

Fred Treves, Waimarama

There are two of us, me and Able Seaman Bowdory
he's sixty – oldest man on board.
I'm in charge – Forward Fire Fighting Party.

Never seen so many ships, destroyers, cruisers,
all grey in bright sunshine.
The attack comes at sunset.

Stukas like banshees falling from hell.
Clan Ferguson goes down
Men burning alive
as she slides under the waves – so quick.

Put on my buoyancy suit.
We've lost three ships – I'm on my knees.
'Dear God, Our father – strong to save.'

Can't remember the rest. Hear my voice
shake. Out of the shadows
Bowdory speaks, *Eternal Father strong to save*

Whose arm doth bind the restless wave...
I'd pray too but I'm too old
to get on my knees, he says.

Lt Commander Roger Hill, HMS Ledbury

After a U-boat attack has damaged her
HMS Nigeria turns back for Gibraltar.
With far too many destroyers
escorting her, in my opinion.

We're attacked by high level bombers
combined with a low level torpedo attack.
Clan Ferguson on my starboard side blows up.
Empire Hope is all on fire.

Convoy in disarray.
Several ships going the wrong way.
With a loud hailer I go alongside
get them going in the right direction.

Almeria Lykes, an American owned ship,
her captain a bit stroppy says he's
going back to Gib.

Tell him he doesn't have a hope
without an escort.
If he joins the others
he'll be in Malta lunchtime tomorrow.
Comes round like a lamb.

I see *Ohio* lying still.
Her captain Mason, seems cheerful.
They've put out a fire,
set up emergency steering gear
but have no means of navigation.

I offer to put a dim light on my stern.
I'll lead you. So they join in.
Soon we're belting along
at sixteen knots.

I order hot soup, stew, cocoa
to be served to all my crew.
Apart from those manning the phones
the rest sleep at their stations.

Fred Treves, Waimarama

It's dark.
I can't sleep
Think I hear men
from *Clan Ferguson*
calling for help.

BH Skilling Second Mate, R M Simon Third Mate, Glenorchy

It's all over for us when the engine room
is hit port-side.
Captain Leslie orders 'Abandon ship'.

Mr Skilling
Port-side lifeboats all blown away
So I get starboard boats into the water
take charge of number 3 boat.

Mr Simon
I do my duty – to check
all 124 personnel are on the boats
Can't find the Chief Engineer.

The engine room is flooded.
He'd never wear a life jacket
I can account for most of the others.

I throw all secret books overboard.
Report to the Master
All right Mr Simon: You go now.

I ask him to come with me.
Life is just beginning for you.
I am remaining as mine is finished.

I tell him this is ridiculous.
His life as master is as valuable
to the country as mine is.

Mr Skilling
I look for No. 1 boat and the ship's doctor.
Need him to take care of the wounded.
Then we go back for the Master.

He refuses to leave his ship.
You have proved yourselves a wonderful crew.
I am proud of you.

Set your course for the land
May God see you arrive safely.
Goodbye and good luck.

Roger Hill

As we round Cape Bon
the sky lights up.
Tracers tearing through the dark.

Star shells bursting
as E-boats attack the convoy.

On our own with the *Ohio*
we've missed most of it.

Wairangi, Santa Elisa, Glenorchy,
Almeria Lykes all sunk.
HMS Manchester has flooded engine rooms
and she's on fire.

We lead *Ohio* back into line
to the remnant of the convoy.
I say a silent prayer.
Don't know if anyone's listening.

Fred Treves, Waimarama

A horrendous night, the 12th of August.
Emergency turns to port and starboard.
Our sister ship, *Wairangi*
vanishes in a sheet of flame.

Like us she's carrying high octane spirit,
ammunition, bombs, shells
and food for Malta.

There's a bit of a lull.
I go to the saloon.
Men have been at the liquor locker.
Many beyond recall.

John Jackson, Junior Radio operator, Waimarama

It's Thursday morning, I'm in the chart room
when Lieutenant Withers, Liaison Officer, says
'Jacko, I reckon we'll be in Malta
in four or five hours.
We'll be all right'.

We hear aircraft approach.
Run for our action stations
port-side of the bridge.

As he steps out
there's a tremendous
whoosh. A solid wall
of flame comes between us.
I step back.

Capt David R MacFarlane, Melbourne Star

We're showered with debris,
a deadly rain of metal
from the stricken *Waimarama*.

Our machine gun post knocked over
by a piece of steel plate.
Nearly kills a naval rating
but he ducks out of the way.

The sea a mass of flame
We've kept close station
so pass through *Waimarama's* death pyre.

I order helm hard to port
jump down from the Monkey Island
to save myself from getting burnt.

I order everyone forward
in case I have to get them off.
Coughing, blinded by smoke.

Air impossible to breathe,
all the oxygen's gone.
We choke and gulp

for what feels like hours
– can only be minutes
as the flames disperse.

Fred Treves, Waimarama

Dawn light shakes me awake.
We're back at action stations
when the bomb hits the deck.

I'm blown into the stores.
Bowdory on top.
I think we're going to die.

72

He gets up, runs out
on deck. I follow.
Petrol cans roar with flames.

We're listing to starboard. I think
of *Clan Ferguson*. Run port-side
dive head-first into the sea.

Swim as hard as I can.
I must get clear before she explodes.
Smoke billows.

As I look back. Bowdory's on a raft.
Being sucked into the fires – no chance of escape.
He can't swim. I cannot go back.

Arms out-stretched.
I turn on my side,
swim away.

Another man in the water
wearing a life-jacket, crying
I swim over – tell him to keep calm.

Roger Hill, Ledbury

At 7.30 on 13th August
a dozen torpedo planes
come in low from the port beam
and a flight of Ju88s
out of the sun.

A stick of bombs lands on *Waimarama*
I have never seen such an explosion.
Flames six times the height of my mast.

A signal from the Admiral
'*Get survivors, but don't go
into the flames.*'

Surely nobody can have survived
but as we approach
there are heads bobbing,
black with oil in the water.

I put down a whaler.
to pick up all she can find.
I call through my loud-hailer

to the men in the water,
First I must get those nearest the fire.
They shout back
That's fine, sir.

The fire is spreading outward
over the sea, even to windward.
It's a grim race.

I'm up on the bridge
heat blistering every surface.
Put my hand over my beard
afraid it might catch light.

My sailors jump into the water
held by straps as they pull men
into landing nets. They are badly burnt.

We gather up all we can find
about forty of them.
Thank God, I can't see anymore.
I'm going astern.

The coxswain calls up the voice pipe
'There's another man over there, sir.'
Coxswain all I can see is flames and smoke.
'Sir I saw him raise his arm.'

John Jackson, Waimarama

I run out onto the port side
thick black smoke and bangs
as the ammunition explodes.

Our ship surrounded by flame
except for a small patch of water
where men are swimming.

I can't swim
but I jump feet first
over the side.

The water's full of wood
and bits. The fire
breathes closer.

I can't get any air.
A young cadet swims up
Jacko, lie on your back.
Don't move. I'll tow you.

Drowning men always struggle.
So I tell myself not to.
Slowly, very slowly
he pulls me away.

A great spar of wood
floats past.
Can you grab that?

I heave myself on to it,
tell him to carry on.
Young Freddy Treves – such a brave lad.

Off he goes
towards the great bulk of *Ledbury*.
She's put down a whaler.
They're dousing her with hoses.

I'm with the cook
who calls
They're going to leave us.
They haven't seen us.

Ledbury is picking the whaler up.
I blow my whistle,
shrill with panic,
wave my arms.

Ledbury comes back
through the flames
to get us.

Captain Fred N Riley, Brisbane Star

Ohio just ahead of us
when she's hit - comes to a halt
I'm forced to throw my helm over
order reverse engines
to avoid a collision.

Empire Hope blows up.
like a furnace.
Clan Ferguson disappears
in a mushroom cloud
of smoke and falling dust.

Charlie Walker, Chief Bosun's Mate, oil tanker Ohio

Sun low on the horizon.
Sky coming alive with stars.
Binoculars to my eyes
I'm searching the darkening clouds.
The yell "Look out, lads, torpedo astern."

DEMS Gunner, Ohio

I'm flung off the gun platform like a rag doll.
A few moments of stunned silence
then all my muscles tense

for the coming explosion.
The afterdeck's ripped open
like a peeled back sardine can.

Captain Dudley Mason, Ohio

We've a hole in our port side
wide as the entrance to the Mersey tunnel.
The pump room's ablaze.

I give the order 'finish with engines'.
Our priority is to put out the fires.
The air attacks continue.

John Dalgleish, Midshipman, Glenorchy

I'm one of the last off
All that's left is a raft
for seven of us to cling to.

Our salvation an Italian E-boat
they're decent enough
considering they bombed hell out of us.

Fred Treves

H.M.S Ledbury looms over us.
A small wooden boat. An officer
in naval uniform grabs my hands.

Ledbury's still under attack.
Try to keep out of the way.
Nineteen of us have survived.

That's ninety men left behind.
Tell myself I'm one of the lucky ones.
But I should have saved him.

Captain David R Macfarlane, Melbourne Star

In a brief lull I return to my day cabin
thinking I might sit down.
A hole gapes in the roof

A six inch shell
embedded in the steel deck below
still intact and unexploded.

Thirty six of my crew missing
Lost over board
as we went through the blaze.

Captain Henry G Pinkney, Port Chalmers

Have caught tin fish
in starboard paravane.

Request advice
on getting shot of it
before it explodes.

Commander Gibbs, HMS Pathfinder

Cut paravane wire.
Swing helm hard over
No.
Wait.

Suggest unshackle
clump chain for'ard
To take pressure off paravane

Then cut wire
That should do it
Then get the hell out of it
Good luck

Captain Henry G Pinkey, Port Chalmers

We need more than luck.
Going astern.

Drawing paravane clear
if we can just slip the gear.

We're seized, lifted
like a child's toy boat
as the torpedo explodes

Thank God it was on the bottom
and us clear enough.

Captain Mason, Ohio

We've re-joined the convoy
– the end of the line
on account of our defective steering.

A dicey moment when *Waimarama's* hit
With our kerosene tanks blown open
any flames would finish us.

Constant air attacks.
A Ju88 crashes into the waves
by our bow – by some mischance,

to my disbelief it bounces
onto the fo'scle with a terrific crash.
Bits fall all around us.

A signal from Ledbury
Am going to assist Manchester
Will return later.

Penn comes alongside.
We attempt a tow.
It's hopeless.

The tail wagging the dog
as we drag the destroyer
round with us.

With the *Ohio* disabled
I ask *Penn* to take my crew.
Spare them the afternoon's bombing runs.

Apprentice Desmond Dickens, Dorset

Their bombers coming straight at us
screeching lower and lower.

They let go their bombs
Our ship lifts out of the water.

Captain J C Tuckett, Dorset

Struck aft by heavy weight bomb.
Engine room fills with water.
Hold ablaze from end to end.
Signal *Bramham*
'Am abandoning ship'.

Roger Hill

We're two hours picking up survivors
Forty-five of them, one dead.
I signal the Admiral,
Short of fuel.
Thirty miles astern of convoy.

A private attack by Ju88s
all to ourselves.
We shoot one of them down.

Another sadness the discovery
Our survivors come
not only from *Waimarama*

but also the *Melbourne Star*
Each ship with three hundred and fifty
on board and all we have are forty four.

We come up to the *Ohio*
                    lying stopped
The *Penn* dropping depth charges.

Half a mile away
Dorset also lies still
with *Bramham* at her side.

I broadcast to my crew
We are continuing with the convoy.
Got to get PQ17 out of our system.

Tell *Penn's* captain I can take *Ohio* in tow.

Captain Mason, Ohio

I have to insist,
to anyone who will listen,
it should be possible

to get her to Malta.
Is it hubris on my part
to regard her as the most important?

Captain Fred N Riley, Brisbane Star

A life on the ocean wave.
A home on the rolling deep.

Still managing eight knots
despite the damage to our bows.
Still on our tod. We limp
through Tunisian coastal waters.

Ah now – an enemy aircraft
come to take a look.

But we are in French waters
Neutral territory for both of us.

This does look like a bombing run.
All gun crews – hold fire.

Let's see if he's serious
That was rather close.

Leave me with my masthead intact
There's a good fellow.

Either he's got no torpedoes
or he's a gentleman.

Off he goes. An Italian gentleman
What did I tell you?

Lieutenant Symes, Naval Liaison Officer

We should have shot him down.
I doubt the Luftwaffe
will be as conscientious
in observing French neutrality.

Signal Station, Hammamet

You should hoist your signal letters.

Captain Fred N Riley Brisbane Star

Please excuse me.

Signal Station, Hammamet

You should anchor.

Captain Riley Brisbane Star

My anchors are fouled.

Signal Station, Hammamet

You appear to be dragging your bow and stern anchors.

Captain Riley Brisbane Star

I have no stern anchor.

Signal Station, Hammamet

Do you require salvage?

Captain Riley Brisbane Star

No
(never mind the matter of the hole).

Signal Station, Hammamet

It is not safe to go too fast.

Captain Riley Brisbane Star

(Oh piss off.)
Hoist all signals.
Let's leave them confused.

Captain Riley Brisbane Star

Here they come again
Patrol boat this time.
Stop? Not on your life
or mine.

Ah – I think they just fired on us.
Stop all engines.

Vichy Officer

I must insist you follow us
You are in French waters.
You are in our custody.

Captain Riley Brisbane Star

But first gentlemen
allow me to be hospitable.
I have the finest whiskey
of all Ireland
or wine, or cognac
whichever you prefer.

Please come to my cabin.
I must insist.
This war – such a terrible business,
but as captain of this vessel
I have to tell you
we are set to continue.

Vichy Officer

You must accompany us

Captain Riley Brisbane Star

I take it you are a seaman
are you not?

Vichy Officer

This is true.

Captain Riley Brisbane Star

Then you will understand my difficulty.
I beg you to be a brother seaman.
Forget you saw me and let
my ship proceed?

Vichy Officer

You may have my word.
We will let you pass.

Captain Riley Brisbane Star

I do have one request.
One of my crew is injured.
If you could take Corfield ashore
I'd be most grateful.
Vichy Officer
Goodbye Captain.
Bon voyage – safe voyage.

Captain Riley Brisbane Star

Oh most unhappy day.
We have a periscope
trailing after us again.

Could be a submarine.
We'll find out soon enough.

Naval Liaison Officer

You do realise the enemy knows
our position. I'm monitoring
Italian frequencies. They keep
reporting our progress.

We have no chance of making Malta.
When we leave the French coast
that sub will blow us up.

Sea transport officer and Chief Officer

You should listen to him, sir.
No sense in going to our deaths.

Captain Riley Brisbane Star

I'll have none of your pessimism.
Gentlemen we are going to Malta.

Crew members, Brisbane Star

No sense in going to our deaths.
He should scuttle the ship.
We can be prisoners of the French.

Captain Riley

The Vichy don't feed their prisoners
or so people say. Not to mention
the shame of giving ourselves up.

Crew members

No sense in going to our deaths.
He should listen to us.

Captain Riley

Tomorrow morning we'll have
air cover from Malta.
We're keeping to our course.

Jim Perry, formerly of Empire Hope

Once we're on board the *Penn*
they take care of us.
Cook gives everyone a hard boiled egg
on a slice of bread.
Not bad once you've picked the mould off.
You can help yourself to a ship's biscuit
from a large tin.
There's over a hundred of us on *Penn's* deck.
Many with that blue dye they use for burns.

Carpenter Norman Warden Owen, formerly of Deucalion

We're sixty miles from Malta.
The *Ohio* dead in the water.
Her master calls us together.
We're to board the *Ohio*.
Her decks a mass of wreckage
we need to shift.

Better the merchant navy
than the RN. We're the ones
who know the drill.

There are enough of us.
We come from *Santa Elisa*
The boatswain from *Waimarama*

A contingent from the *Melbourne Star*
and us - ruffians from *Deucalion*
with our captain, Ramsey Brown.

He works like a galley slave
handling winches and lines.
I'm glad to follow his example.

They're going to try two destroyers
alongside, a makeshift trimaran
with *Penn* and *Bramham*.

Able Seaman

I'm more than tired, keep seeing things,
friends who died on previous convoys
reaching out to shake my hand.

None of us speak above a whisper.
You'd think the enemy might hear.
So eerie I wonder if I've died.

Just haven't noticed.
Keep checking my heart.
Still seems to be beating.

Roger Hill

The Doc arrives on the bridge
as I'm drinking the lunchtime lime juice.
It's too hot to eat. He looks done-in.

Quietly he says to me
What about giving the lads some Benzedrine
you could have some too?

I'm tempted but,
what goes up must come down,
Will there be a reaction later on?
After you've been pepped up?

His reply so soft
 I have to lean forward to hear him.
It'll hit you tomorrow.

Neither of us know where we'll be.
No guarantee we'll have reached
Malta. Better leave out the speed.

An afternoon of *Ohio's*
slow progress, as *Penn* and *Bramham*
carry her forwards.

I long for darkness
but fear another dusk attack
will finish us.

It doesn't come.
Instead a glimpse of white cliffs.
Everyone on board cheers.

The coastal defence open fire on us.
Never heard such language on my bridge
the air crackles blue with our indignation.

We switch on recognition lights,
flash coloured lights for night
but the thud of shells continues.

I signal on full power
to Malta *For Christ's sake stop*
firing on us.

A few more rounds
then
silence.

We stay at action stations.
I give them permission to sleep
except the man on the phone.
Director's crew take it in turns
to check he's awake.

My Sub's asleep standing up
his head folded forwards
onto the chart table.
He'll get a stiff neck
but I let him be.

At dawn as daylight arrives
I walk the upper decks.
My sailors sprawled
hunched in their duffle coats.

Their friends' legs or backs
make pillows.
Sunburn shows on their stubbled faces.

They lie peaceful as children.
Not one of my crew lost,
not a single casualty.

I'm so proud of them
– glad no one's alert
to see me awash in this moment.

John Jackson, formerly of Waimarama

I'm with *Melbourne Star's* fourth officer.
He's seen plenty of action,
says he'll see me right.

When we get into port.
we'll both have to find
a new ship.

Only get a few days survivor's leave
Won't last long
Not with the amount of booze

he plans to get through.
He stops talking abruptly.
His eyes that have seen too much.

How he stares and stares
over my left shoulder
as if at a ghost.

There she is. Paint blistered
from her sides – safe in harbour
the *Melbourne Star.*

Roger Hill

Malta's great ramparts built to withstand
the Turks resound with playing bands,
the thump of drums echoes back towards my ship.

I berth her in French creek.
Look in on the wounded.
Get some dope from the doc.
Strip off my clothes
before going down into a deep deep sleep.

Harbour

Lt Commander Roger Hill, HMS Ledbury

I wake in the evening's cool;
I've slept all day,
right through the visit of the Admiral.
Best not to wake him.

A bath feels glorious after a week in the same clothes.
My white uniform crisp and unfamiliar as I climb
the rocky path to the Ops room.

I apologise for leaving *Ohio* to try and find *HMS Manchester*.
Admiral Leatham is brisk.
Don't worry about that, you did well.
The ships that reached Malta
already half emptied of their cargoes.

Ohio: the vital tanker,
the Commodore's ship. *Port Chalmers,*
Brisbane Star and *Melbourne Star.*
The *Rochester Castle*:
She was hit and caught fire but arrived with most of her cargo,
and five hundred and sixty eight seamen have survived.

Leatham turns to the chart.
We have a report, an Italian merchant ship coming south.
When can you be ready to sail?
The war continues.
In about an hour, Sir.

Aftermath
Lt Commander Roger Hill, HMS Ledbury

In company with *Penn* and *Bramham*,
we sail with sixty surviving seamen.
I'm on the bridge when my knees start to shake
so hard I have to clutch the rails
to keep upright.

A thousand miles to Gibraltar.
Just us three destroyers
no other protection.

I hurry to my cabin
concerned lest my crew see
the state I'm in – am violently sick.

Too long at Sea

For much of the route they'd noticed bits of debris floating on the surface, then suddenly they saw a patch of orange. Fraser [Beaufort's navigator] took out his binoculars and had a closer look. They were, in fact, oranges, hundreds of them, bobbing about on the surface – the remnants of Operation Pedestal.

Fortress Malta, James Holland

Voices in the night,
a heavy tread on the stairs.

This morning there's a man at breakfast.
He's thin with brown skin.

I wish he wouldn't keep staring.
Mam keeps saying,

Pass your father the bread, and
I couldn't get any butter.

He's eaten half the loaf.
Doesn't he realise there's a war on?

Shouldn't he be in uniform?
Suddenly he announces,

I have something for you.
I follow him upstairs.

In the bedroom his dark leather suitcase
with its label, J Honeybill.

A strange smell when he opens the lid –
damp, like seaweed.

Is this where he keeps his uniform?
And something clinks. A gun?

He sighs and mutters,
It's spoiled – gone wrong.

In his hand a white
lump with a crust of blue grey mould.

Not out

Shadows at twilight
lengthen across the pitch
just trees, not souls,

nor anything
like a man,
in a handful of breeze

making the leaves
dance and murmur
their lost song.